Michel Muszynski

PRICING
A SOURCE
OF PROFIT
OR LOSS

ISBN-13: 978-1508798408

Selling prices... How to fix them? How to change them? How to adjust them? What is price differentiation and how to take advantage of it? What is revenue management? And how to use dynamic pricing in the modern business world where... there are no prices any more (in the classic meaning of this world)?

All precise answers and 10 business cases - discussed and illustrated.

Table of content:

Instead of introduction: price and quality 3
Strategic meaning of the selling price 5
General rules of fixing prices 8
Demand curve 13
Practice of defining prices by classic methods 15
Changing prices in time 17
Discounts 20
Prices fine adjustment 21
Conjoint analysis 23
Differentiation of prices 25
Yield (revenue) management 28
Capacity reservation 31
Dynamic pricing 33
Appendix... 38
Index 40
Author.. 41

Instead of introduction: price and quality

Potential buyers make their purchase decisions just analyzing products quality. However they also take under the attention the price of products which is examined by them with reference to their personal spending capabilities, to prices of competitors and also to the operating cost (and sometimes even to the possibility of re-selling the product).

Both, quality and price - seen with eyes of customers - are not absolute parameters, but are rather perceived arbitrarily (particularly with reference to the competition). They are also strongly interconnected: perceived quality and perceived price merge together in a so called "perceived value". And just that value decides about the probability of the purchase of product: higher it is, larger are chances of the purchase.

It is convenient to present the value perceived by customer graphically[1], in two dimensions which are the mentioned quality and the mentioned price. This allows to define four possible purchase situations:
- Low-quality (the lack of features of product which could attract the buyer) and high price - what corresponds competitively to the worst position of the seller, qualified usually simply as „rip-off"
- Low-quality and low-price - that position can be called „economy"
- High-quality and high price – this can be found in so called „premium" products, unique enough and not having substitutes
- High-quality and low-price - such position is qualified by customers as „bargain" and gives the greatest probability of sale

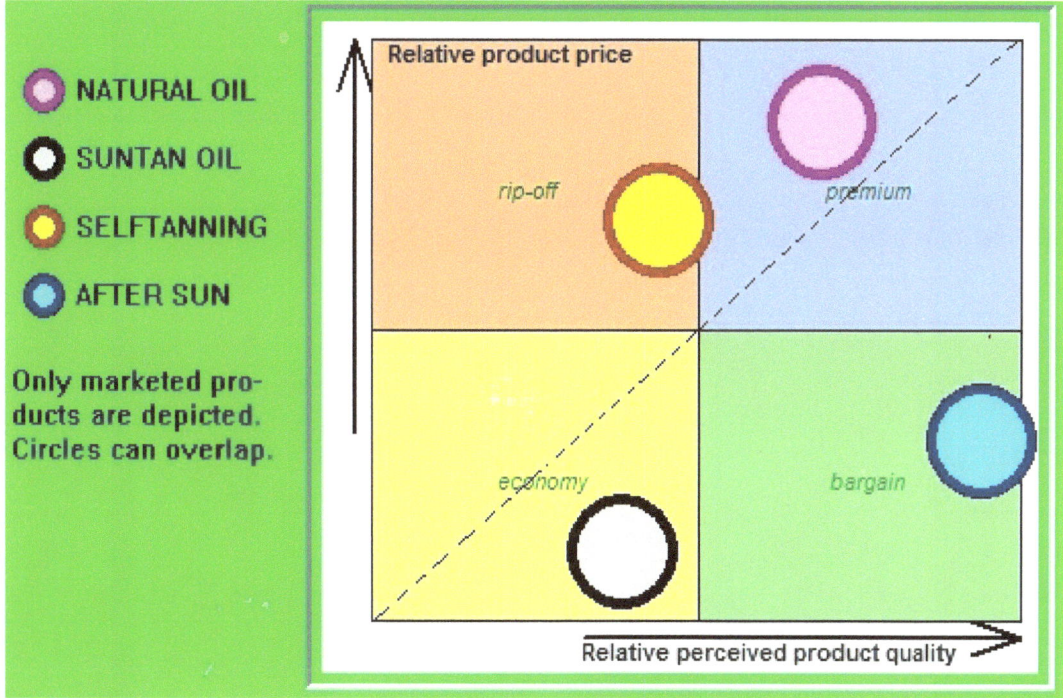

___

[1] In marketing that presentation corresponds to one of possible product positionings.

Here is the two-dimensional matrix: quality/price for the offer of one of manufacturers of cosmetics. It is visible that customers consider his SELFTANNING lotion as unreasonably expensive, although NATURAL OIL- also perceived as expensive - has an excellent quality.

Since selling products which are perceived by customers as being located in the lower right quarter of the above two-dimensional matrix is easy but doing so for goods or services situated in the upper left quarter is tough, the dashed diagonal line shown on the illustration splits it on two zones: of the gain of market share and of the market share loss. This is the first conclusion which can be drawn from the map: quality/price.

A second, extremely important message coming from the above illustration is that high quality products (in previously explained sense) - can be sold more expensively, since customers are willing to pay more for the quality. Price and quality of products are indissoluble.

Strategic meaning of the selling price

„What is the price of this product?" - the response given by the seller to such question has in most of cases a key importance for closing the sale. This shows why price (as part of marketing-mix) is mentioned three - or even four times more often than such elements as advertising, distribution, whether even features of product itself (having also a potential influence on selling - after all).

The selling price is therefore extremely important - and this is a general principle, even in countries generally considered as rich. The famous Wharton Business School published in 1997 results of an research on the reactions of American air carriers after different kinds of the strategic moves induced by their competitors. Those strategic moves have been classified in two separate categories: related to a change of the selling price and other, embracing all remaining cases. It appeared that - among the group of observed airways - a change of the selling price made by a competitor had 75 % of chances of a riposte, while on all another strategic moves of the competition air carriers reacted only in 17 % of cases. What is more, the mentioned riposte on the change of price was almost immediate (only 5 days later, on average), while the reaction on other strategic moves was as slow as 17 days!

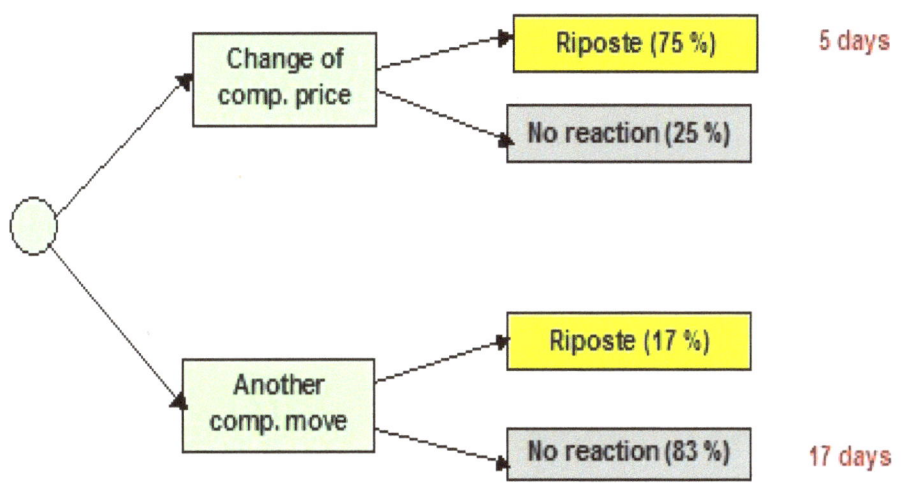

Airways companies reacted on a change of competitors' prices in so firm manner! And they were right: it is easy to prove, that just the change of selling price (and not for example a reduction of costs or even an increase of sales) influences most strongly the operating profit. Such statement can seem unbelievable, proving its truth is however easy – as easy as showing that it is universal, completely independent on the type of corporations and even on the market segment.

This crucial importance of the selling price in profit generation results from the following elementary formula describing corporate financial results:

Profit = Sales * (Price - VariableCost) - FixedCosts,

where „Sales" are calculated in volume (not in dollars) as number of units of product and expressed in pieces, kilograms, gallons, hours of work, etc.,

FixedCosts refer to a whole company, and „*" is the multiplication sign. As an application example[2] of this formula just imagine a company selling monthly 100 pieces of a product at the price of $ 100 a piece. This company has her fixed costs of $ 3000 and an unitary variable cost of $ 60 is associated with each piece of the above product. Putting those values into the formula gives the profit of that company as $ 1000:

$$Profit = 100 * (\$ 100 - \$ 60) - \$ 3000 = \$ 1000$$

Consider now this $ 1000 profit just as a starting situation. Imagine also that the management of the firm succeeds in increasing sales by 10 % (it means to 110 pieces of product) - without changing neither prices, nor costs. This will increase the financial result to $ 1400, which means by 40 %. How large however will become this profit when, keeping the previous sales level (100 units) and the previous costs, the company will increase the selling price by 10 %? In that case profit will jump up to $ 2000, that is twice the previous result. At the end, decreasing the variable cost, and then also the fixed costs, and using the same method (that means changing each of them by 10 %), will show an increase of the corporate profit by, respectively, 60 and 30 %:

Sales	Price	Variable cost	Fixed costs	PROFIT
Starting situation:				
100	100	60	3000	1000
Increase of sales:				
110	100	60	3000	1400
Increase of profit due to 10 % better sales =				40%
Increase of price:				
100	110	60	3000	2000
Increase of profit due to a 10 % higher price =				100%
Lower variable cost:				
100	100	54	3000	1600
Incease of profit due to a 10 % lower variable cost =				60%
Lower fixed costs:				
100	100	60	2700	1300
Increase of profit due to fixed costs reduced by 10 % =				30%

Changing the price has therefore the greatest influence on financial results of corporations. That influence will depend of course on combination of the values of

---

[2] Simple but very instructive, proposed by Simon-Kucher & Partners consulting company.

variables: Sales, Price, VariableCost and FixedCosts in the formula presented above, however it is possible to demonstrate that the influence of Price will be always the most important - or at least equally important as the influence of any of three other remaining parameters. This confirms the importance of the price as an element of the corporate strategy which cannot be overestimated.

However asking managers of contemporary corporations the question about methods they use for fixing their selling prices, causes often their embarrassment. Despite the fact that most of them agree to the necessity of having prices contributing to the highest possible profit, they are less unanimous when talking about details. The most frequent answers given in that matter are:

- The highest possible price („because this generates earnings")
- The lowest possible price („because large sales generate large profit")
- Price similar to the competition („because competition must be right")
- Price fixed by others (for example by the management of the company)

General rules of fixing prices

How to define prices – since they are a so important element of the strategic management and - simultaneously – they cause so many controversies? The problem appears complicated enough, however it is generally admitted that defining prices should take into account three factors – different and often contradictory:

1. The market (and therefore the point of view of customers)
2. The own profitability of the seller
3. The competition

The market is described usually by a relation (function) between the selling price and the demand. In case of most of products this function is decreasing (when the price increases, the demand reduces), however well-known are also cases of customers' interest growing along with the price (up to a certain level of price and declining above it). Luxury products behave in such manner as well as other goods (having not necessarily birth-marks of luxury) of comparatively high value, purchased by the buyers who consider that prices cannot be too low for a fair quality.

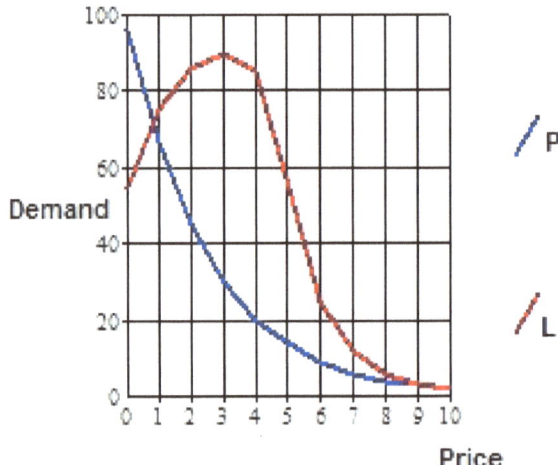

This is illustrated on the graph above, where luxury products are designated with the letter "L", while other, popular (common) products – with "P". The demand is expressed for a unit of time: it is visible that in case of both kinds of products demand for large prices decreases, approaching asymptotically the zero. In practice the use of curves shown here proves difficult, since a precise definition of their shape demands very detailed market analyses. Due to this an approximation of the straight line is usually made here for popular products (and broken straight line in case of luxury products):

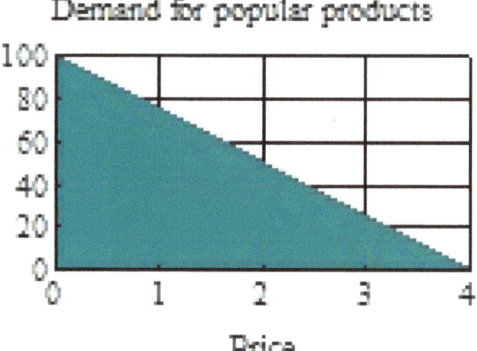

Demand for popular products

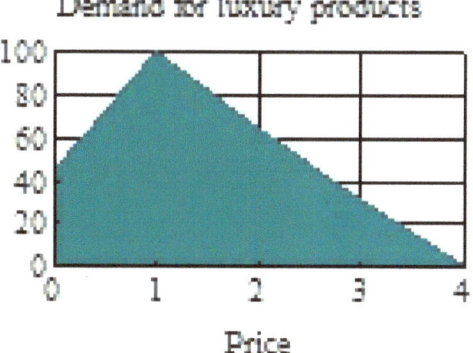

Demand for luxury products

Further considerations in this book will remain limited to popular (common) products only. The next illustration demonstrates the dependence of market demand on the selling price, approximated just with a straight line. The reader will remark the point PM of the intersection of the graph with the horizontal axis, called maximum price: this is the highest possible price, above which selling the product will be no more possible (the demand will disappear). Another point DM on the illustration is called maximum demand: this point describes the interest of the market for the product when it is sold at the lowest possible price (1 ¢ for example). A mathematical expression of this dependence Demand = f(Price) will be a simple linear equation:

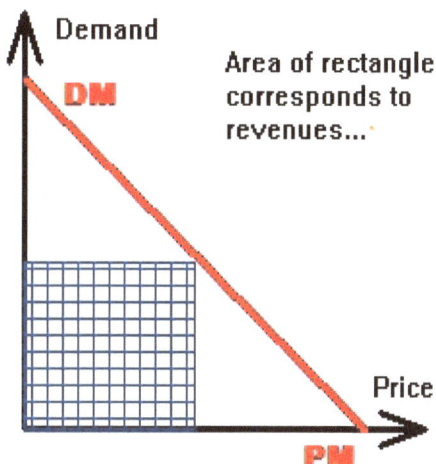

$$\text{Demand} = (-\,DM\,/\,PM) * \text{Price} + DM$$

where „Price" is the current price, „Demand" the corresponding demand and signs „*" and „/" are - respectively - the multiplication and the division.

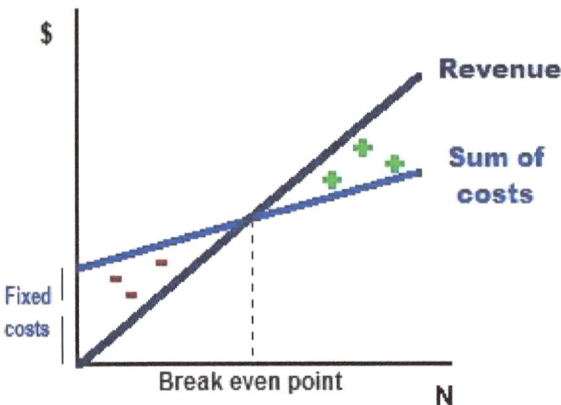

The second factor defining the selling price is <u>the profitability of the seller</u>. Its calculation is based on the dissociation of costs related to a product on fixed (FixedCosts independent on the selling volume) and variable (VariableCosts). On the illustration above the red color designates the sum of both such costs and violet color - revenues coming from product sales. The point marked as "x" is the breakeven point: above the breakeven point the company realizes profit and below it - insufficient sales generate the financial loss. Usually, for the quantitative reasoning, the easiest way is to start from a well known formula presenting the financial results of a corporation as:

$$Profit = Sales * (Price - VariableCost) - FixedCosts$$

In the breakeven point Profit = 0:

$$0 = Sales * (Price - VariableCost) - FixedCost$$

and therefore the sales corresponding to it:

$$X = FixedCost / (Price - VariableCost)$$

How the break even changes when the selling price increases?

Since "Price" is in the denominator of the last formula, the break even point decreases.

The reasoning presented above allows a very easy calculation of the Price = P_{BE} corresponding to the situation when the company makes neither losses nor profit:

$$P_{BE} = VariableCost + FixedCosts / Sales$$

or

$$P_{BE} = VariableCost + FixedCostsFor1PieceOfProduct$$

P_{BE} has an important practical meaning, as it defines the lowest possible price below which selling is no more profitable. Its computation requires however making an hypothesis about the volume of sales, or - to put the thing in financial terms –

knowing in advance how large part of company fixed costs should be covered by selling one (every) piece of product.

Assuming in the first approximation that a company practicing the price "Price" is monopolist on its own market, because the competitors are absent the volume of sales of this corporation will equal the whole available demand (Sales = Demand). It is then possible to combine the last formula with the formula describing the relationship Demand = f(Price) shown previously:

Demand= (- DM / PM) * Price + DM
Profit = Sales * (Price – VariableCost) – FixedCosts

and, after making substitution and calculations, it gets out that the financial result of a corporation is a square function of her selling price. This is illustrated on the graph as an upturned parable. The top of this parable corresponds to a so called optimum price P_0:

$$P_0 = (PM + VariableCost) / 2$$

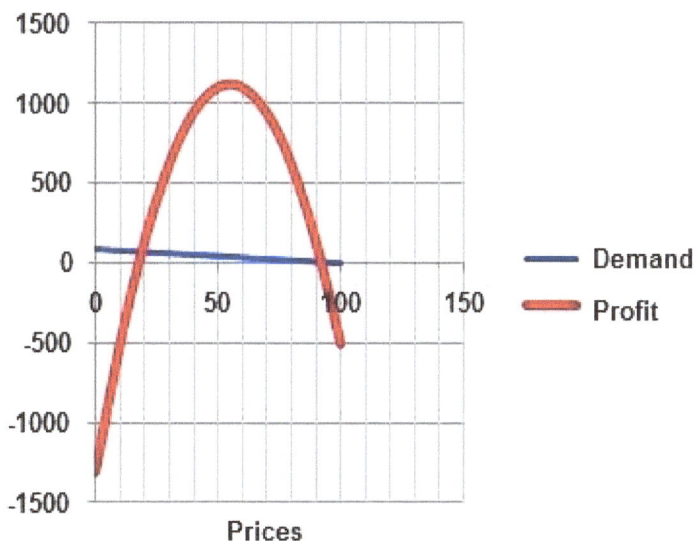

where the financial result of a corporation is the best possible. However "Financial result" does not mean always "Profit" and the formula giving P_0 is not a warranty of profit: in case when fixed costs of the company are very large, she will register a loss nevertheless and practicing the optimum price will simply make her financial result the best possible (the lowest loss). In that situation the top of the parable on the illustration will appear below the horizontal axis.

Although the above conclusions were drew out after approximating the function Demand = f(Price) with a straight line and also after assuming that the competition is non-existent, they have however a fundamental strategic meaning. First they emphasize average ranges of price, since when the prices are low the revenues realized are simply insufficient, and when the prices are high – the sales volume is too limited. Then even in case when the company is not the market monopolist (there is an active competition for company's products) – prices practiced by that corporation should never exceed P_0 - unless the quality of the above products is significantly higher than the quality of her competition[3].

How to calculate a so important strategic parameter as is the optimum price P_0? In most of companies who use nowadays controlling techniques a precise definition of the variable cost VariableCost is not a serious problem. Calculation of the maximum price PM is definitely much more difficult – but nevertheless possible thanks to the market analysis. This usually consists of asking potential buyers of product such questions as: „What is the highest price you would still accept to pay for this?". The response to that question can be however considered exclusively as an information about the intention of potential customer – and certainly not as an actual observation, which unfortunately reduces the reliability of calculation of a so defined maximum price PM.

This ends the discussion about defining selling prices from the point of view of the market as well as of the corporate profitability. Mathematical expression of influence of the competition on those prices is considerably more complex and difficult. However, it seems logical to accept that those prices should depend on quality of products perceived by customers. In other words, prices practiced by different and working on a common market suppliers should be proportional to what customers think about their respective products and such statement is relatively easy to be applied in practice when proceeding to a simple market analysis. The expression „perceived quality" should be however considered as being completely subjective: a „better" commodity or a „better" service satisfies simply a larger number of concrete needs of potential buyers.

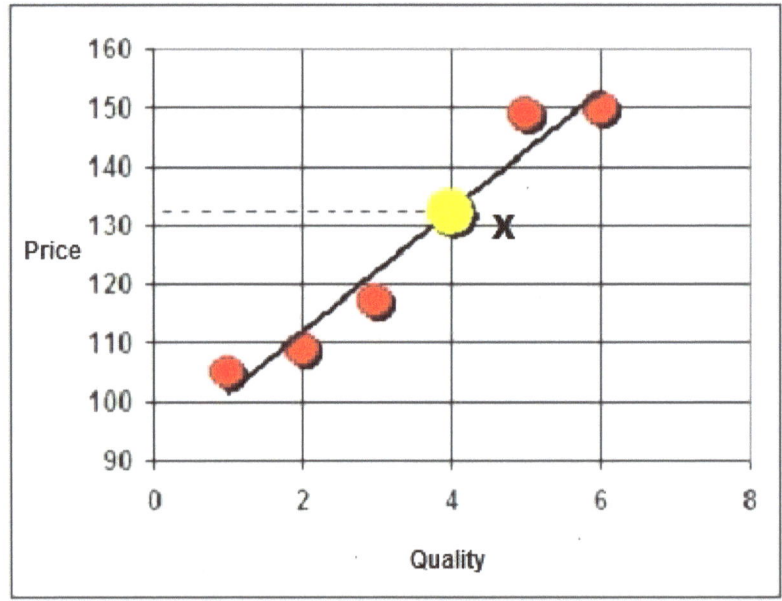

Quality and price perceived by customers for a few products of different competitors, compared with the price and the quality of a selected product marketed by a certain company (designated as "X"): prices are approximately proportional to qualities. This illustration has been prepared after interviewing a group of 120 potential product users.

---

[3] Yet company's products are similar to the products offered by the competition.

Demand curve

Although finding very precisely the shape of the relationship Demand = f(Price) is not absolutely necessary for estimating PM (and then the optimum price P_0), a few words now about the market analysis. As long as prices are concerned its easiest way is asking the potential product buyers the question: "What is the highest price you would still accept to pay for this?". The calculation of the maximum price PM is then based on the assumption that an interviewed person accepting the price X would also (and even easier) accept any lower price, i.e. X-1, X-2, X-3, etc. Adding up the number of all responders for a given price level X-1, X-2, X-3, etc. will help in defining the relationship between the demand and the price (and thus the shape of the demand curve).

CASE:
Here are the answers given by 14 potential customers after asking them the question "What is the highest price you would still accept to pay for this product?":

Person:	a	b	c	d	e	f	g	h	i	j	k	l	m	n
Price $:	9	15	7	8	7	13	15	11	14	10	9	11	12	8

Plot the Demand = f(Price) curve...

Solution:
Since the potential customer "a" accepting the price $ 9 would also accept $ 8 and $ 7, then:

Accepted PRICE	$ 7	$ 8	$ 9	$ 10	$ 11	$ 12	$ 13	$ 14	$ 15
Person a	X	X	X						
Person b	X	X	X	X	X	X	X	X	X
Person c	X								
Person d	X	X							
Person e	X								
Person f	X	X	X	X	X	X	X		
Person g	X	X	X	X	X	X	X	X	X
Person h	X	X	X	X	X				
Person i	X	X	X	X	X	X	X	X	
Person j	X	X	X	X					
Person k	X	X	X						
Person l	X	X	X	X	X				
Person m	X	X	X	X	X	X			
Person n	X	X							
DEMAND	14	12	10	8	7	5	4	3	2

Assuming the sample of 14 respondents is large enough and representative of the whole market, the relationships Demand = f(Price) is:

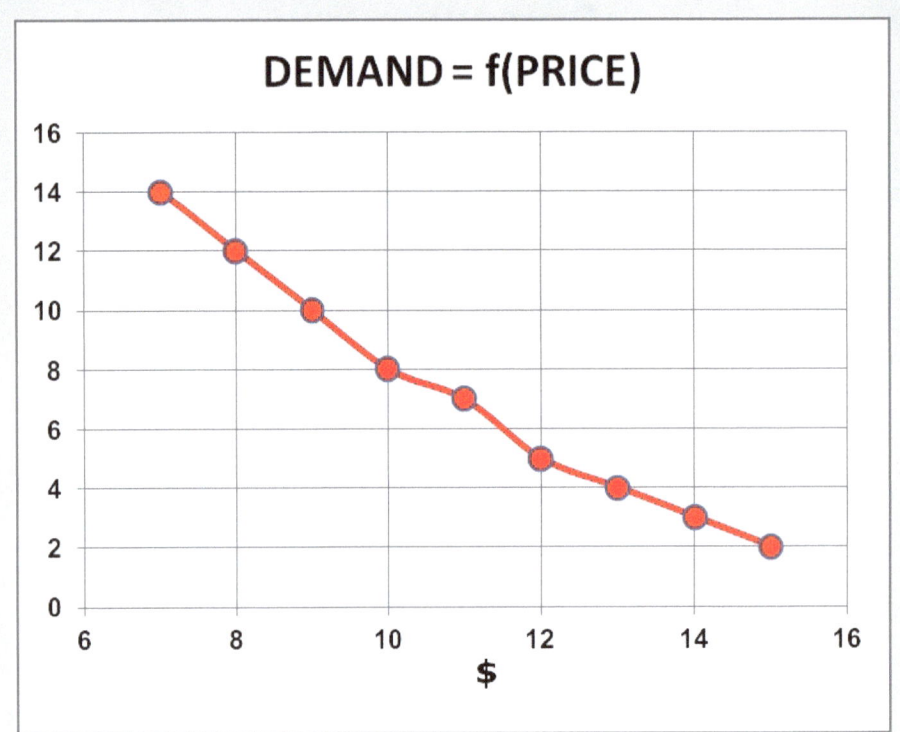

DEMAND = f(PRICE)

Based on this illustration the maximum price will be – by extrapolation - $ 17.

How easy is to change the selling price? This depends on the slope of Demand = f(Price) curve: steeper it is, larger will be the resulting change of demand. Usually this is described by what is called "price elasticity[4] of demand":

Very elastic demand   **Inelastic demand**

---

[4] **The full formula is: e = (ΔDemand / Demand) / (ΔPrice / Price), where ΔDemand is the change of Demand resulting from the variation of Price described as ΔPrice – and e is measured at a given Price corresponding to a certain Demand point of the curve.**

Practice of defining prices by classic methods

The above considerations show that, when defining the strategy of pricing, three following parameters have the highest importance:

1. The optimum price P_0, making the best financial company's result (either profit or loss)
2. The breakeven point and corresponding price P_{BE}, essential for avoiding financial losses
3. The relationships between perceived quality of the product and prices of market competitors

In most of cases, prices practiced by the majority of companies will have values situated between P_{BE} and P_0 (P_{BE} as the limit between the profit and loss and P_0 as the price corresponding to the potentially highest profit):

$$P_{BE} \longleftrightarrow P_0$$

The segment $P_{BE} - P_0$ can be however wide enough. A more precise definition of the selling price will be still a matter of the adjustment between perceived quality of the product and competitors. That adjustment should rely on making an estimation of quality of product perceived by customers, on comparing that quality to the competition and (finally) on defining on that base an "honest" price P_H which the market could find normal. This brings up to plotting the function Price = f(perceived Quality) and finding P_H through interpolation (or extrapolation) for a certain perceived quality of the product whose price has to be fixed.

CASE:
SUCCESS Corp. manufactures and sells small plastic garden swimming-pools. Their unitary variable cost is $ 400, while monthly fixed costs of the whole corporation are $ 2000000. The company estimates the possibility of her sales on 2000 pieces a year, in spite of having three competitors. The first from them - Alpha practices a selling price of $ 1800, the second - Beta $ 2000 and the third called Gamma - $ 1700. SUCCESS Corp. sent recently among potential buyers a questionnaire in order to estimate qualities of different market offers perceived by them. According to different answers collected, the swimming-pools manufactured by Alpha are rated 2 in a relative five-points scale, by Beta - 4, and products offered by Gamma - 1. Simultaneously, customers perceive the quality of SUCCESS Corp. offer as approximately 3. What selling price should consider this company, knowing that the market maximum price for plastic swimming-pools certainly does not exceed $ 5000?

Solution:
The optimum price P_0 = ($ 400 + $ 5000) / 2 = $ 2700

The price corresponding to the breakeven point
$$P_{BE} = \$ 400 + \$ 2000000 / 2000 = \$ 1400$$

The "honest" price P_H (from the graph shown) = $ 1900

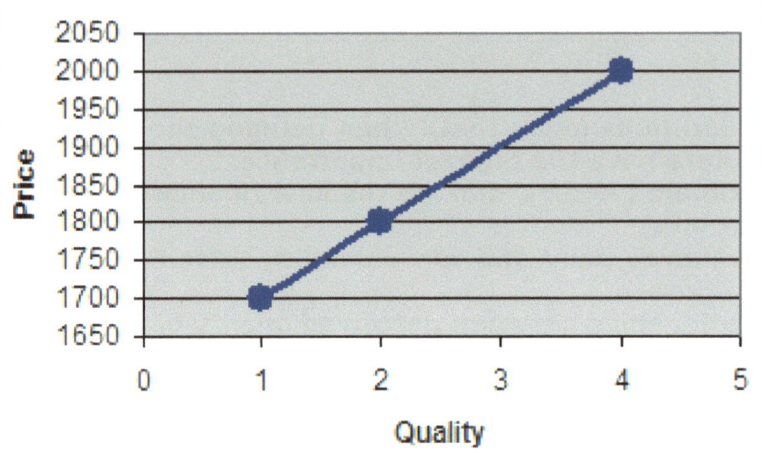

▶ **SUCCESS Corp. should consider a selling price around $ 1900.**

To be continued...

The above example represents the most common situation: $P_{BE} < P_H < P_0$. However other cases are also possible and will be discussed further, in the chapter devoted to prices fine adjustment.

The practical calculation of the "honest" price P_H by the above described method is unfortunately often difficult, because the function Price = f(perceived Quality) can have a not clearly defined graphic form (for example a huge dispersion of points corresponding to different competitors) and also because obtaining a reasonable reliability of results of the market research appears often infeasible. Particularly, customers exposed to the marketing interview and having to answer the question: „How good is for you the quality of the product X (in 0 to 5 scale)?" are not in the position to respond, because the word „quality" is too abstract for them...

Changing prices in time

It is matter of fact that prices are not fixed forever and during the process of their definition the company can also take into account an evolution of them in time. Particularly the penetration strategy consists of introducing the product for a song and then gradually increasing its price. Inversely, in the screaming strategy, after introduction the product on the market it is first very expensive, then - only some time later - reaches a low price (acknowledged by most of customers as „normal"). Observations of the market show that screaming strategy is used more often than the penetration, since lowering prices is much easier than raising them.

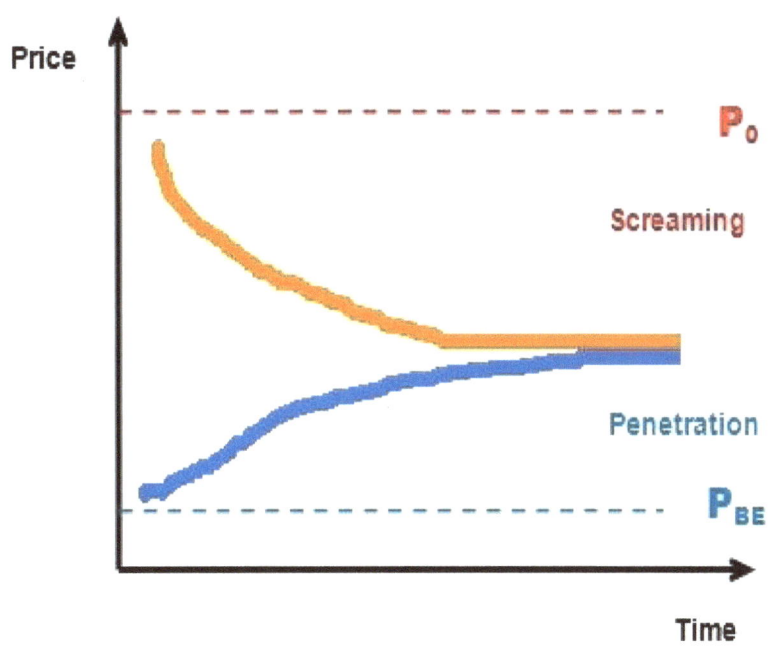

This asymmetry can be explained by the game theory. When two competitors (called WE and THEY) realizing each $ 100 of profit, act on the market, a simultaneous increase of prices by both players improves often profits of every from them. However an increase of prices by one only of the competitors causes in general a reduction of his profits and a simultaneous improvement of the financial result of the second market player. Understanding this very well, neither WE nor THEY wants to execute the first move - since if the second player do not accept to imitate him, he will lose money. The things are quite different in case of prices reduction. The competitor making the first move in that direction in general gains at the expense of the second player. This is why, to avoid the diminution of his own profits, the second competitor also reduces his prices, what - finally – causes sometimes the decrease of financial results of both enterprises simultaneously:

THEIR PRICE

	No change	Rise
Rise	WE: 140 of profit THEY: 80 of profit	WE: 120 of profit THEY: 120 of profit
No change	WE: 100 of profit THEY: 100 of profit	WE: 80 of profit THEY: 140 of profit

No change   Rise   OUR PRICE

In case when both competitors could arrange themselves regarding a common rise of prices and trust each other - they could both win. Such arrangement would be however a self-evident violation of the antitrust law and would strike customers' interest.

What are the reasons which push to use either screaming or penetration price strategies? Screaming is appropriate when:
- The seller (and buyers) consider his product is better than the product sold by competitors
- The seller wants to avoid perception of his product as having a low quality

Strategy of penetration works well if:
- The seller variable costs are low compared to his competition
- The seller introduces his product on the market full of competitors who started selling similar products before him
- The seller expects the competition to arrive on the market very soon
- The seller has accumulated an important stock of unsold goods (overstock)
- If his product gains value when it has a large number of buyers (for instance computer e-mails are only useful when many people use computers)
- If this product is susceptible on the effect of experience which means its variable cost decreases when the number of units of product sold increases[5]

There is a close relationship between changing prices in time and their level fixed regarding previously discussed P_{BE}, P_H and P_0 - since "introducing a product for a song" (penetration) or "expensively" (screaming) means almost always[6] comparing its price to the competition (and thus to the honest price P_H). Therefore the strategy of penetration corresponds usually to using prices from the range $P_{BE} - P_H$ and the strategy of screaming from the range $P_H - P_0$:

---

[5] See the book of M. Muszynski – „Multi-business: from diversification - to corporate holding".
[6] This is not true only if there are no competitors.

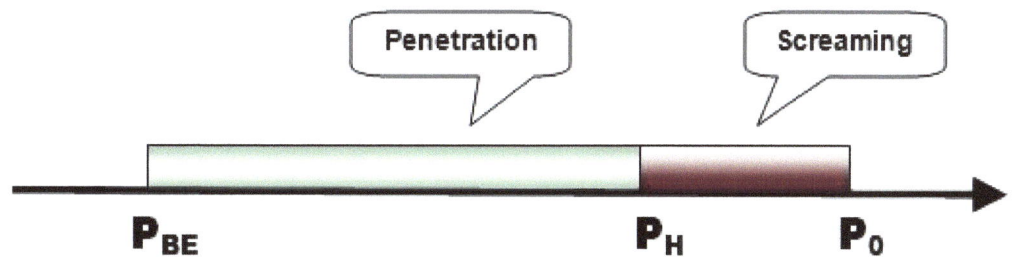

CASE:
Let's come back to the previous case – where:
$$P_{BE} = \$ 1400 < P_H = \$ 1900 < P_0 = \$ 2700.$$
Suppose the company is a newcomer on the market which has been shared till now by three very aggressive competitors. What selling price this company should fix?

Solution:
For a market newcomer the strategy of screaming is out of the question, therefore a price in the range $ 1400 - $ 1900 will be appropriate.

Discounts

Discounts are a special sort of pricing. How do they influence seller's profit?

Many people imagine a 10 % discount reduces the financial result by 10 % but this is quite wrong. Discounts are calculated against the full selling price, while margins depend also on the variable cost of product. Suppose a company selling a product at $ 100 per unit. Suppose as well the corresponding variable cost is $ 90. Giving a customer a 10 % discount reduces the selling price of product to $ 90 – which makes seller's margin (profit corresponding to 1 unit of product) shrinking to... zero!

Before discount	After discount
Selling price = $ 100 Variable cost = $ 90 Margin (profit) = $ 100 - $ 90 = $ 10 which is $ 10 / $ 100 = 10 %	Price = (100 % - 10 %) * $ 100 = $ 90 Variable cost = $ 90 Margin (profit) = $ 90 - $ 90 = $ 0 which is $ 0 / $ 100 = 0 % !

Of course an as high as $ 90 variable cost compared to a $ 100 selling price is not a common situation, however a X percent discount reduces the margin always by more than X %, since the variable cost is never null.

CASE:
A company manufactures and sells about 5000 lifejackets a year. Their regular selling price is $ 180 per unit, the unitary variable cost is $ 120 and the company supports $ 165000 fixed costs per year. A new customer is interested by buying an additional batch of 800 lifejackets but he asks "a very important discount". How large it could be?

Solution:
Assuming all fixed costs are covered by other regular buyers, the lowest possible selling price will equal the unitary variable cost and therefore the unitary discount could perhaps reach $ 180 - $ 120 = $ 60 which gives:
$$\$ 60 / \$ 180 = 33.3 \%$$
However, in case the conditions offered to the new customer have to be the same as those of regular buyers, he has to support the same proportion of fixed costs:
$$\$ 165000 / 5000 = \$ 33 \text{ per unit of product}$$
and therefore the discount offered to him has to be reduced to:
$$\$ 60 - \$ 33 = \$ 27 \text{ per unit}$$
In that case the relative discount will be:
$$\$ 27 / \$ 120 = 15.0 \%$$
Of course this 15 % discount doesn't offer to the seller the opportunity for making any profit.

Prices fine adjustment

Let's come back to the discussion about defining the selling prices based on three values: P_{BE}, P_H and P_0. As it was already said, usually $P_{BE} < P_H < P_0$ but other cases are also possible. For instance what if P_H is lower than P_{BE} or higher than P_0?

No matter how large the honest price P_H is, when the price corresponding to the break even point P_{BE} exceeds the optimum price P_0, the product is definitely not profitable. It cannot be profitable since a company using P_{BE} makes neither losses nor profit and with P_0 she realizes by definition the best possible financial results. In case $P_{BE} > P_0$ those "best" results are therefore negative (losses) – which is of course a good reason for stopping (cutting) the product:

$$P_{BE} < P_0 \; !!!$$

Another situation is when $P_{BE} < P_0 < P_H$: just because P_0 makes company's financial results the best possible, selling more expensively is certainly not a good idea.

And finally in case of $P_H < P_{BE} < P_0$ only the second inequality can be considered (since for all prices below P_{BE} the product will be not profitable). The segment P_{BE} – P_0 will however exceed prices of the competition, therefore using this prices range will be possible only if the strategy of screaming has to be applied.

If...	... then price strategy
$P_{BE} < P_H < P_0$	P_{BE} < penetration < P_H or P_H < screaming < P_0
$P_{BE} < P_0 < P_H$	Price should be $\leq P_0$
$P_H < P_{BE} < P_0$	P_{BE} < Price < P_0 – possible only if screaming
$P_0 < P_{BE} < P_H$	Don't sell (product is not profitable)!
$P_0 < P_H < P_{BE}$	Don't sell (product is not profitable)!
$P_H < P_0 < P_{BE}$	Don't sell (product is not profitable)!

In the end a few words about the "final touch" during the prices adjustment process. It concerns what is called "price barriers": they are the thresholds corresponding to significant changes in customers behavior. The most typical is $ 100: it is much easier to sell at $ 99.95 than at $ 100.05 – whereas the difference between these two numbers seems really insignificant (¢ 10) and corresponds to only about 0.1 % of this price! Another "price barrier" is observed at $ 10: it is the reason why so many small value goods are priced at $ 9.95 or $ 9.99. Even though their cost for customer is in fact $ 10, their buyers remember it as "nine dollars something" and it seems cheaper...

Fixing a price a little below the "price barrier" usually helps selling, however in some cases also gives the impression of a bargain. Luxury goods (for instance expensive watches) are therefore priced $ 2400 rather than $ 2399.95.

There are three competitors on the market of jogging dresses, all three offering products of very similar quality: SPORT-COMFORT, FAST STYLE and AVANTI. This last company wants now to define her price strategy and has discovered that SPORT-COMFORT sells his own products for $ 300, while FAST STYLE for $ 280. According to AVANTI, the higher price of jogging dresses possible to be accepted by customers is $ 400. The variable cost of one dress carried by this company is $ 100. What should be her price strategy: close to $ 250, close to $ 280 or close to $ 300?

Solution:

Let's calculate the optimum price first. According to the formula, this is the sum of the variable cost of AVANTI and of the maximum market price, divided by two:

$$P_0 = (\$ 100 + \$ 400) / 2 = \$ 250$$

Since this maximum price is the price where the company yields the best possible financial result (it will be worse for any higher price) and both AVANTI competitors sell nevertheless more expensively (perhaps they have higher variable costs?), then a price close to $ 250 should be the best solution.

Conjoint analysis

Difficulties encountered when fixing the selling prices by classic methods are the reason for a more and more frequent usage of another technique of defining the "honest" price P_H, called „conjoint analysis". This (computerized) method - although making also use of questioning the potential buyers - does not consists of a direct plotting the graph of the function Price = f(Perceived quality), but rather of calculating P_H through making by interviewed persons several subjective choices: product A whether product B, B or C, C or A...

When Jessica Smith was planning to go to Lisbon for a short holiday, the travel agency proposed her three different airplane tickets: priced at 320, 240 and 200 dollars. She chose of course the cheapest one and then found out that it had been associated with a loss of two days from her week-long only holiday – as two, lasting a couple hours each, changes of airplanes were necessary: in Frankfurt and then in Madrid. The medium priced flight seemed considerably shorter, however the plane was leaving at... 3 A. M. Finally only the most expensive ticket offered the quality of travelling which fully pleased Jessica - simply its cost was unfortunately as high as 320 dollars! If she could treat conditions of traveling aside from the price, surely she would choose just this solution. If instead she could be concerned only with the price, she would decide on the most cheaper ticket. However because the travel agency was not in the position to offer her a direct flight for 200 dollars, she had to treat the price and the quality of traveling as two marketing variables mutually dependent: cheaper was the travel, worse had to be traveling conditions...

How Jessica should solve this problem? The only method would be defining a comparative common scale for both variables. This would rely on defining what relative value different prices and different conditions of traveling are for her. That value would be calculated in a certain (although the same for both variables) scale and results would be able to be presented for example as follows:

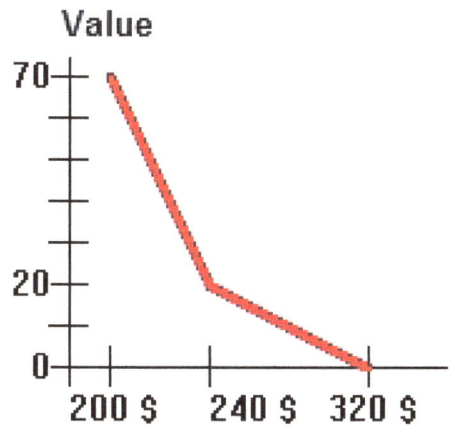 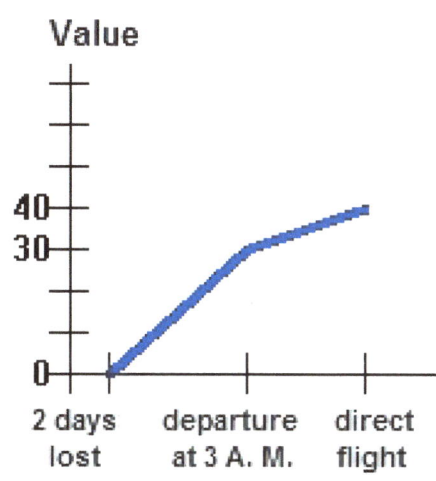

If the above illustrations present the real Jessica's preferences, it is then clear that prices are for her globally more important than conditions of traveling, since the difference between the best and the worst solution in their case is 70, and for the second of variables - only 40.

Further, when having the values of two described here marketing variables for each kind of travel tickets, it is easy to add them up, calculating like this the total value of every from those tickets. For example, in Jessica's scale, the 320 dollars flight will be globally worth 0 + 40 = 40 points, the intermediary price travel 20 + 30 = 50 points and the cheapest ticket 70 + 0 = 70 points. Jessica should choose of course this last solution since it has the highest value.

The above constitutes just the rule of the conjoint analysis - a very efficient tool of products management and, particularly, of defining their prices. In this method a choice between several products being in competition is given to a group of potential customers. They have to decide which of those products - having different prices and different qualities - they prefer. For example:

Product A

120 HP
Sport body
$ 76000

OR

Product B

100 HP
Limousine
$ 58000

On the basis of choices (answers) made by customers, value of each variable is qualified in a common agreed upon scale and, after adding up, the total value for each of products is calculated. Because the probability of purchase of every from them is proportional to this value, it is easy to make a prognosis concerning their sales (and even their respective market shares). For example:

Product A: total value 150, probable future market share 30 %
Product B: total value 100, probable future market share 20 %
Product C: total value 250, probable future market share 50 %

More, conjoint analysis makes also possible defining the most desirable combinations of mentioned marketing variables necessary for improving those future market shares. For example, because the agreed upon value of the price and the car engine power are expressed in the same scale, it is easy to estimate what admissible rise in price corresponds in eyes of customers to an increase of engine power of 10, 20 or 30 HP. Or, how expensive can be a car in sport version, comparing to limousine – having the same technical parameters? In other words, thanks to conjoint analysis the company can easily exchange one marketing variable of the product with another, in order to maintain or even to increase her selling price and to improve simultaneously her sales.

Differentiation of prices

The method of price definition presented so far is univocal, that is the price has the same value for all of product buyers. The modern strategic techniques use however more and more often another method called „differentiation of prices". This name qualifies methods where the price for a similar (or almost the same) product is not the same for all customers, but depends on their willingness to pay. A typical example are airplane tickets sold in two or even three classes (economic, business and first), whereas the above classes are still divided on zones depending on the form of payment, the time-limit of ticket validity and the date of trip. Such manner of doing constitutes a specific kind of the strategic differentiation of products, where a similar (or almost the same) commodity or service is perceived as having different attributes of quality by market segments having different financial capabilities (and therefore also different perceptions of the selling price).

To explain the strategic sense of the differentiation of prices, let's observe that the optimum price P_0 defined by an enterprise corresponds on the first illustration below to the revenue expressed by the area of the rectangle formed by multiplying P_0 by the demand. The zone (triangles) not belonging to this area, but being found under the graph Demand = f(Price), is lost for the enterprise. In other words, it results from the illustration that a certain increase of the company revenue could be possible under condition of a better fulfillment of the area under the mentioned graph. It is easy to achieve this when using not only one but two (or more) different selling prices of the same product for different segments of customers:

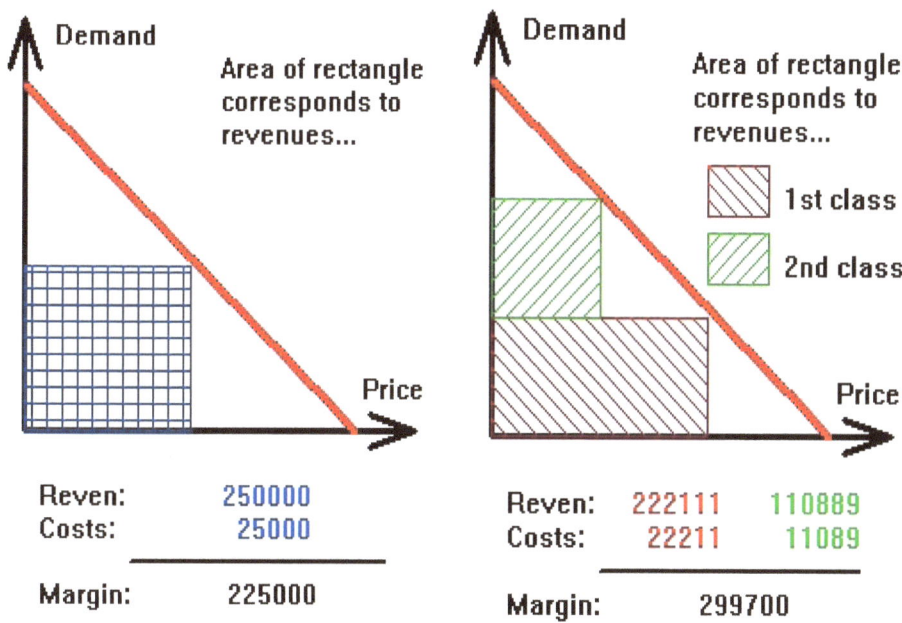

Of course those segments cannot mix. It is therefore necessary to separate them by a so called "fencing" (erection of barriers). In general it is achieved thanks to a (sometimes rather artificial) differentiation of the product for every from those segments (e. g. lounge soft chairs in first class compartments of railway carriages – while hard seats in the second class). Another manner of fencing can be making the selling price dependent on the place (different fares of hotels located in different places but adherent to the same chain), on the quantity of purchase (more means cheaper), on time (tickets purchased just before aircraft departure are more expensive than when they are purchased a month in advance), etc. Here is an English text relative to those questions, written in... 1849:

By no means not due to the necessity of investing a few thousand of pounds some railway lines in Europe exploit third-class carriages with wooden benches and no roof: they want simply that passengers of second-class do not travel third. In other words they do not tease modest people because they have something against them, but for terrifying the haves. Thus really, these lines make the same to first-class passengers: they are inconsiderate for poor persons and avaricious for more rich, simply to stifle as much money as possible from rich people!

Fencing has to be efficient. Here is an example used by an aircraft carrier:

	First class F	Economy class Y	Discount class H or Q
Price	$ 1200	$ 500	$ 300
Comfort: seat size	Large	Normal	Normal
Comfort: service	Full meal	Light snack	Light snack
Early purchase of ticket	No	No	30 days in advance or more
Refundable (if not used)	Yes	Yes	No
Minimum stay at destination	No	No	7 days
Typical user	Business	Holiday Business	Holiday

After comparing two last illustrations above, it should be clear that, because the strategy of prices differentiation helps to increase revenues, it makes better margins and higher profits. It is easy to imagine an even better optimization through an introduction of larger number of prices for different market segments (instead of only two). The main drawback of this technique is its negative perception by different customers who – in case they are asked to pay different prices for the same (or almost the same) product - can feel deceived...

CASE:
New hotel facilities have to be opened in Harrington in Florida. Situated only just 300 feet seaward, they have 52 rooms on four floors as well as an restaurant and are the only hotel in that city. Recently hired management staff of this enterprise is working out her price strategy for the coming period. Two options are considered: one unique rate for all 52 rooms or splitting the hotel on two categories: standard and executive - on two top floors, from where the view of the sea is the best. The variable cost of a room – no matter in which category - will be $ 120 per night, the maximum possible price $ 300, while the maximum demand (corresponding to a price close to zero) 120 rooms daily. What should be the price strategy for this hotel?

Solution:

Assuming an one common rate for all rooms and the situation of monopoly, P_0 = (PM + VariableCost) / 2 = (\$ 300 + \$ 120) / 2 = \$ 210. At this price level $Demand_{210}$ = - (DM / PM) * Price + DM = - (120 / \$ 300) * \$ 210 + 120 = 36 rooms, which corresponds to the day's hotel financial result of $Demand_{210}$ * (Price - VariableCost) = 36 * (\$ 210 - \$ 120) = <u>\$ 3240</u>.

In case of two different rates (\$ 180 standard and \$ 240 executive) $Demand_{180}$ = - (120 / \$ 300) * \$ 180 + 120 = 48 rooms and $Demand_{240}$ = - (120 / \$ 300) * \$ 240 + 120 = 24 rooms. However because none of rooms of the hotel cannot belong to two described categories simultaneously, therefore in the reality $Demand_{180}$ = $Demand_{180}$ - $Demand_{240}$ = 48 - 24 = 24 rooms. This corresponds to a day's hotel financial result being a sum of results for both categories 24 * (\$ 180 - \$ 120) + 24 *(\$ 240 - \$ 120) = <u>\$ 4320</u>.

▶ The introduction of two different rates, \$ 180 and \$ 240, will increase the financial result of the hotel by 33 %!

Yield (revenue) management

All previous discussions of the strategy of products differentiation during the process of definition of selling prices have been based on the assumption that the enterprise enjoys sufficient productive power (output capacity). In other words it was supposed till now that the company could satisfy without difficulty the whole demand at the selling price she practices. In many sectors of the economy however this is not the case when that demand starts to be seasonal.

For example in the sector of services the seasonality appears as the irregularity of gaining over new buyers and is especially visible in tourism and hospitality industry, where the ratio between the volume of inquiries in different seasons, whether different hours, exceeds often one to hundred. However the productive power of airways, railroads, hotels and movie theaters (cinemas) is constant and little elastic. This opens the problem of its adjustment to a variable number of customers: if the output capacity corresponds to the volume of demand in hot periods – that causes a financial loss another time, but when this productive power is not so large – the tourism and hospitality institutions deprive themselves of profits in periods of prosperity.

For solving this problem more and more companies use "yield (or revenue) management". This name designates a set of techniques of adjusting the demand to output capacities which is a certain variety of described in this chapter method of differentiation the selling prices. The general principle of it is that the prices have to be higher in the period of high demand - than off season. As says the tale, yield management was used for the first time by the owner of a barber-shop in Texas, not able to satisfy the huge demand on Saturdays and having almost nothing to do on remaining days of the week. He decided then to double Saturday prices, cutting them simultaneously by two another time. Visits of customers became more equably arranged in time, larger was also the profitability.

Similarly act now hotels, airways and cinemas, as well as even cruise line, trying to fit the demand to their own output capacities. On the graph below showing the function Demand=f(Price) the yield management corresponds to increasing P_0 to P_Y. This assures the realization of the greatest possible revenues in periods of the highest demand and therefore also yields a maximum profit.

*Cruise lines use
the yield management.*

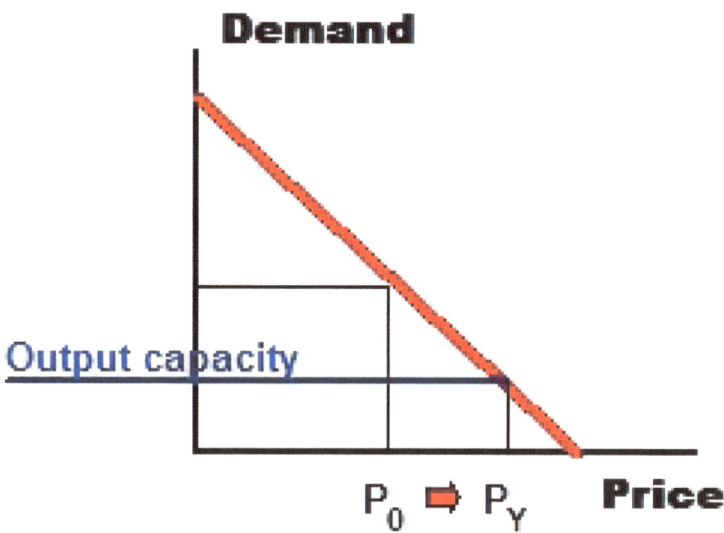

Practicing yield management seems to be very simple. However the basic difficulty of this technique is to fix the price P_Y mentioned above so that the demand is precisely and every day corresponding to the productive power of the hotel, airway company, whether cinema or cruise line. The problem is that demand shows usually some (often very large) accidental fluctuations, which makes the definition of very precise pricing rules quite difficult.

CASE:

A hotel uses the yield (revenue) management. The maximum day's demand (close to zero price) for its services during the week is 400 rooms, while weekends only half of this. The hotel property counts only 150 rooms. Assuming it has no variable costs at all and in the middle of week the maximum price of hotel services is $ 300, what rate this hotel should fix for the week-end: $ 120 per night, $ 150 per night or $ 200 per night?

Solution:

We know nothing about hotel competitors. Assuming they are not very active, the first step consists of calculating the optimum price (there are no variable costs):

$$P_0 = (\$\ 0 + \$\ 300) / 2 = \$\ 150$$

The week-end maximum demand at this price level will be 400 / 2 = 200 rooms, however at a price of P_0 only about half of this (100 rooms). Since the hotel capacity is larger (150 rooms), the best price will be $P_0 = \$\ 150$.

Imagine a company using the price differentiation technique involving two classes (as described in the previous chapter). This price schema is based on two values P_1 and P_2, as well as on two output levels: Capacity$_1$ and Capacity$_2$. Capacity$_1$ is reserved for customers paying P_1 and the difference Capacity$_2$ – Capcity$_1$ is for those who pay the economic price P_2:

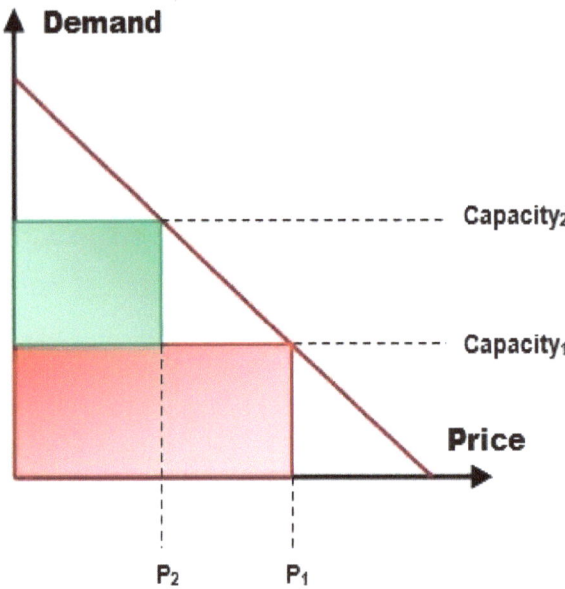

Imagine also that the demand reduces (large red color arrows on two illustrations below) due to an accidental fluctuation – which makes prices and capacities not matching any more:

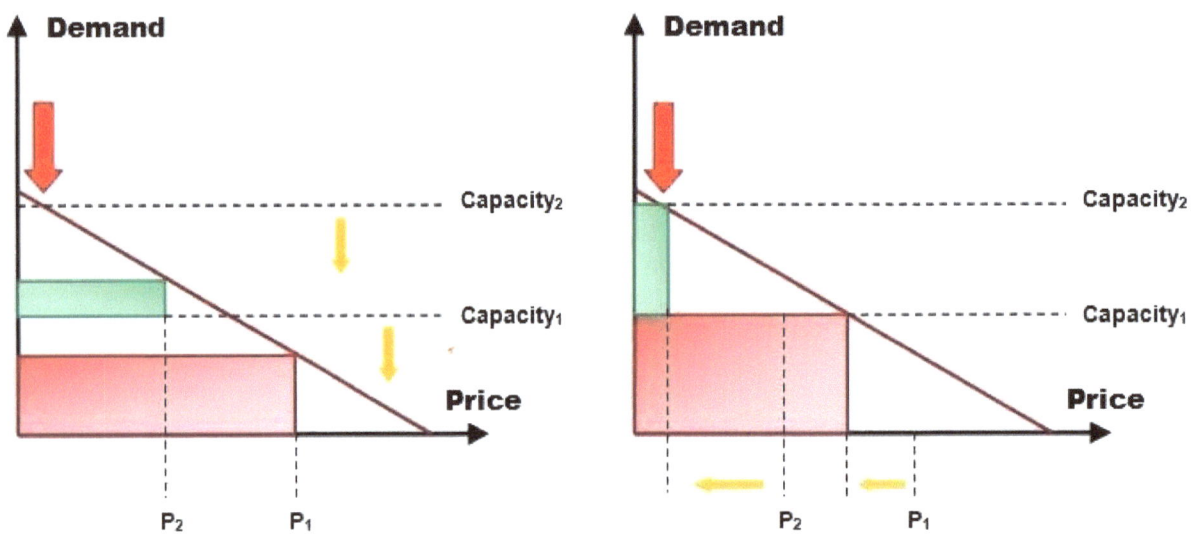

If the company decides to keep the prices P_1 and P_2 unchanged this leaves her capacities unused (see illustration on the left) and to avoid waste she has to modify them. If instead she decides to match the capacities with the new function Demand = f(Price), she has to reduce P_1 and P_2 (right side of the illustration above). In both cases the revenues are of course worse than in the previous situation of a better demand.

The last two illustrations correspond to two possible methods of coping with demand accidental fluctuations, called "capacity reservation" and "dynamic pricing".

Capacity reservation

This first method is also known as "Protection levels" and can be used exclusively when the fencing applied to separate different segments of customers (paying different prices) allows the modification of capacities. This is often the case in airplanes where modifying capacities means simply not offering the same service for different passenger classes (and pushing a tissue separation curtain across the aircraft cabin). This is however more difficult if the equipment and facilities offered to passengers paying not the same fare have to be completely different.

Capacity reservation is based on five assumptions:
1. The selling prices are fixed and the output capacity is not unlimited (i.e. a train or aircraft seat whether a hotel room or a movie theater place sold to a person cannot be sold to another)
2. The inventory is perishable i.e. an aircraft or train seat whether a hotel room or theater place unsold cannot to be sold later
3. Customers paying more buy services usually after clients paying less (for example passengers of business class buy their ticket later than those who plan to travel in economy or second class)
4. The probability of finding a customer paying more is well known
5. From the company point of view it is better to sell a service (airplane or railroad ticket, hotel room whether cruise) cheaper than do not sell it at all

Suppose a customer wants to buy a service several days before the aircraft / train departure or before the date of hotel room rent / movie presentation and he is interested by the economy class (priced at P_2). Is it better to sell him this service now or rather to wait for another passenger who will pay the superior class fare $P_1 > P_2$ – despite the fact this can occur in the future and therefore it is not sure at all? The answer depends on the difference between P_1 and P_2, however because the second customer will be buying not immediately but (perhaps) in the future, an expected value $P_1 * \eta$ has to be used instead of P_1 – with η as the probability of the expected purchase in the time to come. When:

$$P_2 \geq P_1 * \eta$$

then selling the economy class now is preferable - if not, it is better to wait for another customer willing to pay more.

This reasoning can also be used when not one but several economy class customers want to buy but in that case the probability η of finding in the future superior class buyers will depend on their number. This is why η has to be extended to a series of $\eta(1)$ for just 1 customer, $\eta(2)$ for two, $\eta(3)$ for three of them, etc. Of course these $\eta(1)$, $\eta(2)$, $\eta(3)$,... will not have the same values (since it is easier to find in the future two customers than twenty of them) and therefore:

$$P_2 < P_1 * \eta(1)$$
$$P_2 < P_1 * \eta(2)$$
$$P_2 < P_1 * \eta(3)...$$
.....
.....
$$P_2 < P_1 * \eta(x - 1)$$
$$P_2 < P_1 * \eta(x)$$
$$P_2 > P_1 * \eta(x + 1)$$
$$P_2 > P_1 * \eta(x + 2)...$$

Selling the economy class is preferable only starting from x + 1th future customer, which means that x aircraft or train seats, cruise places or hotel rooms have to be protected for clients willing to pay the higher price (P_1). This capacity should be reserved for the superior class and this value is not constant in time but depends on the day of the week, month of the year, different economic factors and also on competition and has to be permanently monitored.

CASE:

A small hotel facilities with only 20 rooms uses the differentiation of prices with P1 = $ 125 and P2 = $ 95. A given day the probabilities of finding customers willing to pay more are:

Number of customers	1	2	3	4	5	6	7	8	9
Probability	98 %	90 %	77 %	60 %	43 %	21 %	7 %	4 %	2 %

How many hotel rooms should be protected for customers paying P_1?

Solution:

When trying the formula: $ 95 ≥ $ 125 * η it is easy to find η = 76 % where the sign of inequality changes from "<" to ">". This corresponds to a protection level of 3 hotel rooms for future customers willing to pay the superior price.

Dynamic pricing

Hotels and airways practice also what is called dynamic yield (dynamic revenue) management. Its very well-known aspect are promotion campaigns called „last minute". Tourist enterprises, having difficulties with selling the last available hotel rooms, aircraft seats or ship cabins, reduce prices in the very last moment - in order to remain always fully booked. Such form of dynamic yield management is universally well-known, however there exist also its inverse variety, consisting of increasing – rather than reducing prices.

The method we are talking about is another manner of coping with demand accidental fluctuations and – contrarily to the method of capacity reservation – can be used even if the fencing barriers separating different segments of customers don't allow the modification of capacities.

Prices fixed dynamically are prices depending on the rate of selling services. This technique is widely used now by hotels selling through the internet when the reservations of their rooms fill too fast. Also airways change constantly prices of their tickets depending on the number of pending reservations. Such selling method is called "dynamic pricing" and, according to its principle, the selling price of product is treated not as a well defined and constant marketing variable, but rather as a freely negotiable parameter, dependent only on temporary fluctuations of the demand and supply:

Data of making reservation:	5.V	12.V	19.V	26.V	3.VI
Observed internet hotel room rate (scheduled check-in date: 15.VI[7]):	$ 125	$ 120	$ 105	$ 130	$ 115

To be able to practice dynamic pricing, a very attentive monitoring of changes of demand is however necessary (and therefore the number of reservations has to be permanently watched). This can be made with the help of reservation curves (usually plotted by computer), such as:

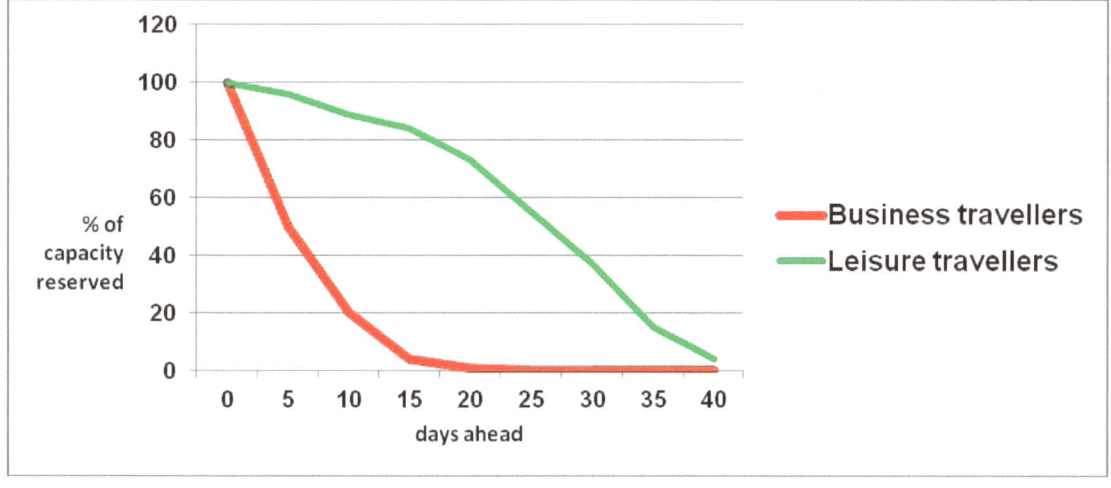

___

[7] Roman numbers designate months of the year.

The next example, shown on the graph, illustrates the case of a small, having only 50 rooms, hotel and presents reservations for 30 days ahead (since today, till to-day+29 days):

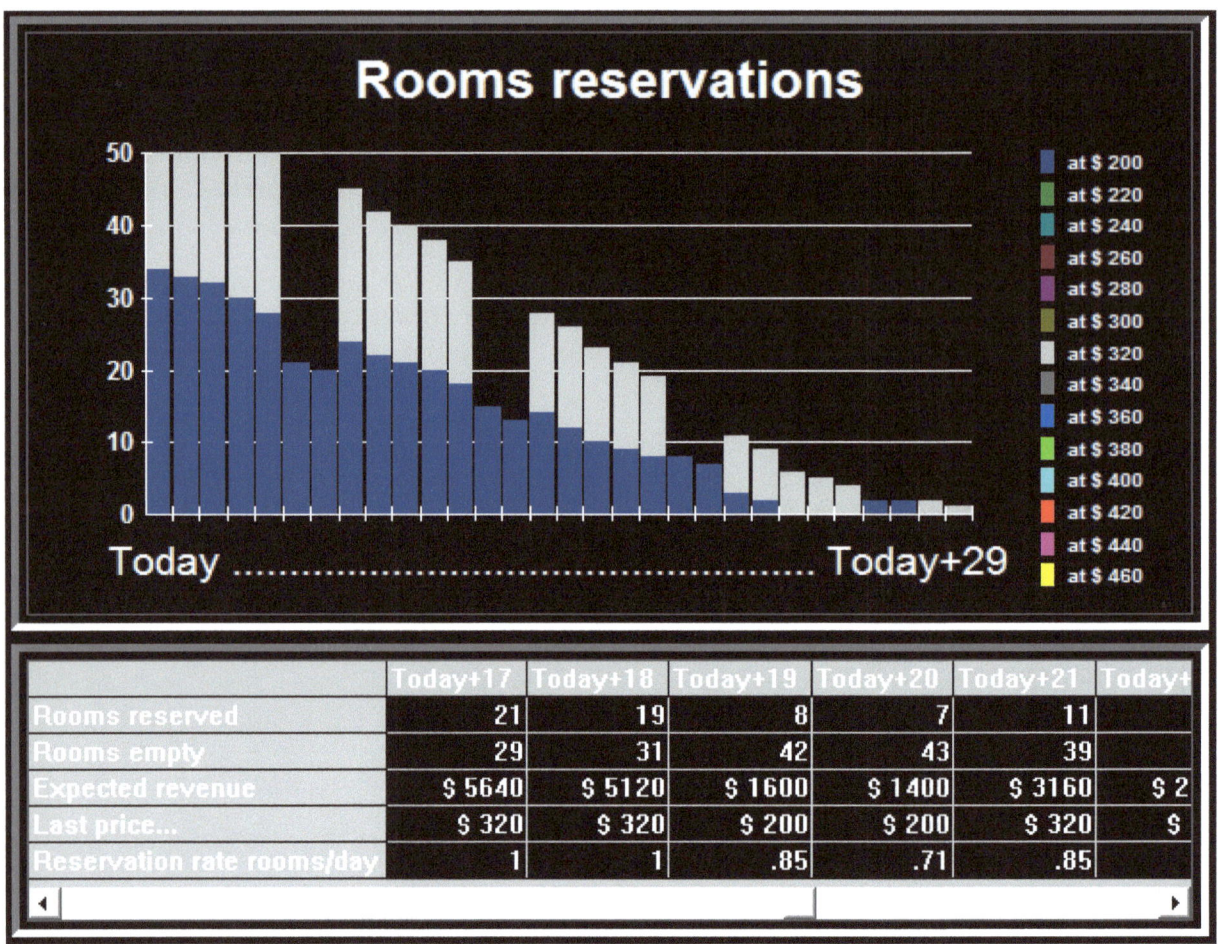

	Today+17	Today+18	Today+19	Today+20	Today+21	Today+
Rooms reserved	21	19	8	7	11	
Rooms empty	29	31	42	43	39	
Expected revenue	$ 5640	$ 5120	$ 1600	$ 1400	$ 3160	$ 2
Last price...	$ 320	$ 320	$ 200	$ 200	$ 320	$
Reservation rate rooms/day	1	1	.85	.71	.85	

First of all on the illustration it is visible that the management of the hotel, observing a very (too) slow increase of the number of room reservations in time, pushed the prices down. That reduction of rates was however clearly too large, since it caused an exhaustion of hotel capacity (50 rooms) not only for today, but also for all four next business days. Attaining a full booking of the property four days ahead (today till today + 4 days) is not a quite good practice and prices could be therefore a little higher (what could help in achieving larger revenues and a better corresponding profit). On the illustration it is also visible that weekend prices of this hotel were too high, as they did not offer any chance on fulfilling the output capacity of the property on the sixth and seventh day of the week.

It is proper to add that the above technique of dynamic pricing, taking advantage of reservation curves, does not take into account a so essential parameter which is the time of staying in the hotel. It appears very often that customers booking rooms for certain days of the week stay in the property longer, than when reserving for other dates. That influences of course hotel revenues and should therefore be considered during the process of prices definition. However not many tourism and hospitality enterprises take this under the attention yet.

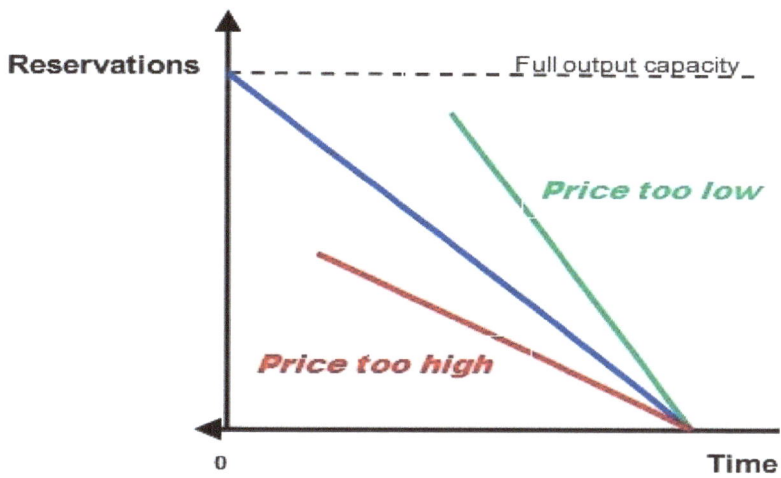

If the price (rate) is too low, the hotel property fills too fast - resulting in the lack of vacant rooms well before planned date of check-in: selling more expensively could be therefore possible. Inversely, if the price is too high, some rooms of the hotel will remain unoccupied.

Another example of dynamic pricing comes from airways. They have similar problems of demand fluctuations in time and face the thread of either flying with empty seats, or "leaving the money on the table" (selling travel tickets too cheaply). The dynamic pricing techniques used to overcome this difficulty apply mathematical formulas based on two assumptions:

1. **The airplane ticket price has to decrease if there are still empty (i.e. unused - not sold) seats**
2. **This price reduction has to be larger when the number of days prior the airplane take-off (i.e. remaining time) diminishes**

Here is a simple example of such a possible mathematical formula (where the index "²" designates "square") with an application:

$$Price = Threshold\ price + (1 + 1/NumberOfEmptySeats) * (Constant - (DaysBeforeTake\text{-}off - 30)^2)/10$$

		20	5	2	1
Threshold price	**400**				
Constant	*900*				
Empty (unused) seats		20	5	2	1
Days before take-off	30	**495**	**508**	**535**	**580**
Days before take-off	27	**494**	**507**	**534**	**578**
Days before take-off	24	**491**	**504**	**530**	**573**
Days before take-off	21	**486**	**498**	**523**	**564**
Days before take-off	18	**479**	**491**	**513**	**551**
Days before take-off	15	**471**	**481**	**501**	**535**
Days before take-off	12	**460**	**469**	**486**	**515**
Days before take-off	9	**448**	**455**	**469**	**492**
Days before take-off	6	**434**	**439**	**449**	**465**
Days before take-off	3	**418**	**421**	**426**	**434**
Days before take-off	0	**400**	**400**	**400**	**400**

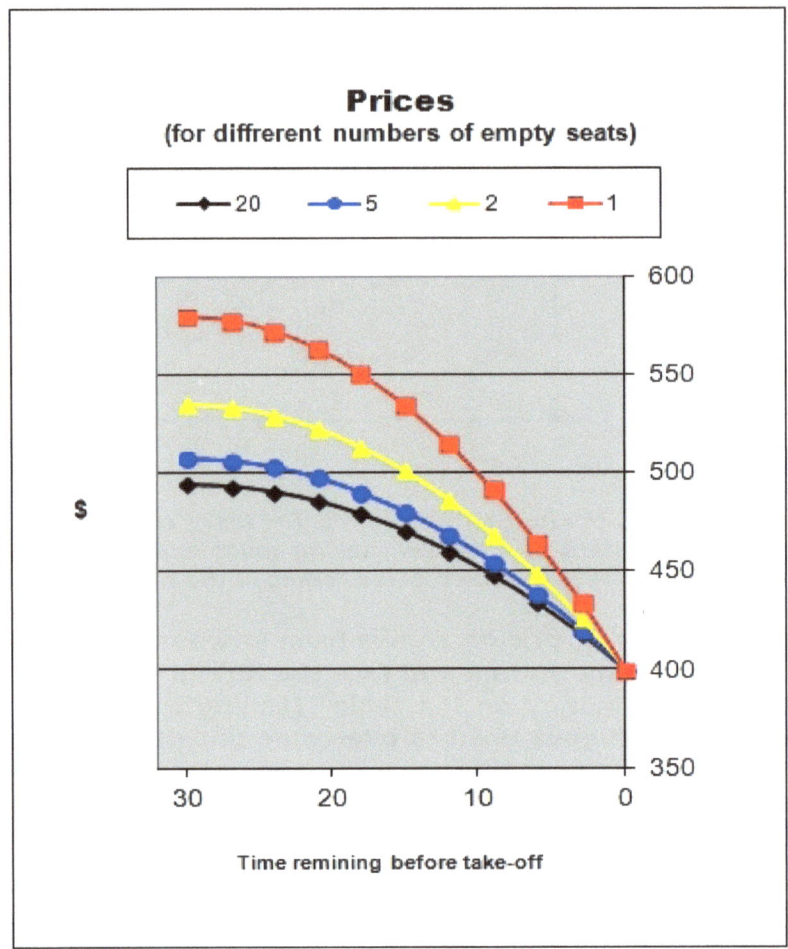

Prices
(for different numbers of empty seats)

Time remining before take-off

Depending on the date when the seat reservation is made the travel price varies from $ 580 to $ 400.

CASE:

A hotel uses dynamic yield (revenue) management and wants to achieve booking close to 100 %. It offers rooms at a promotional price of $ 125 to its best (frequently coming) guests, while the standard rate is $ 250 per night. The capacity of the hotel reaches 500 rooms – and today 420 from them are already reserved for the next week, i.e. seven days in advance. The rate of reservation for standard rooms is 90 every week and for the promotional price 65 every week. During how many days the hotel should still continue to accept promotional price reservations: not at all (no more), 3 days or the whole next week?

Solution:

The unused hotel capacity is now 500 – 420 = 80 rooms. This is less than the week rate of reservation for customers paying higher rate (i.e. $ 250 per night), therefore there is no possibility to consider those who want to pay less. The hotel should therefore stop accepting promotional price reservations immediately.

Although in this book most of Demand = f(Price) curves were supposed to be straight lines, other shapes are also possible. In the next case a broken four-segment line was supposed as an attempt to approximate the hyperbola:

<u>CASE:</u>
A railroad company has started a new fast train with carriages in two different classes: a full meal with beverages is included in the price of the higher of them. Each of those two classes is offered in turn in two sub-categories – "saver" for customers buying tickets at least a month in advance and "regular" for other people. The prices in the 2nd class are: "saver" $ 17 and "regular" $ 40, while in the 1st class: "saver" $ 150 and "regular" $ 300.

Three months after starting this new fast train the railroad company decided to make a review if it (see the illustration below), since the sales of tickets were unsatisfactory: in both classes the sub-category "saver" performed well but very few "regular" tickets were sold (question marks). How it is possible to explain this situation?

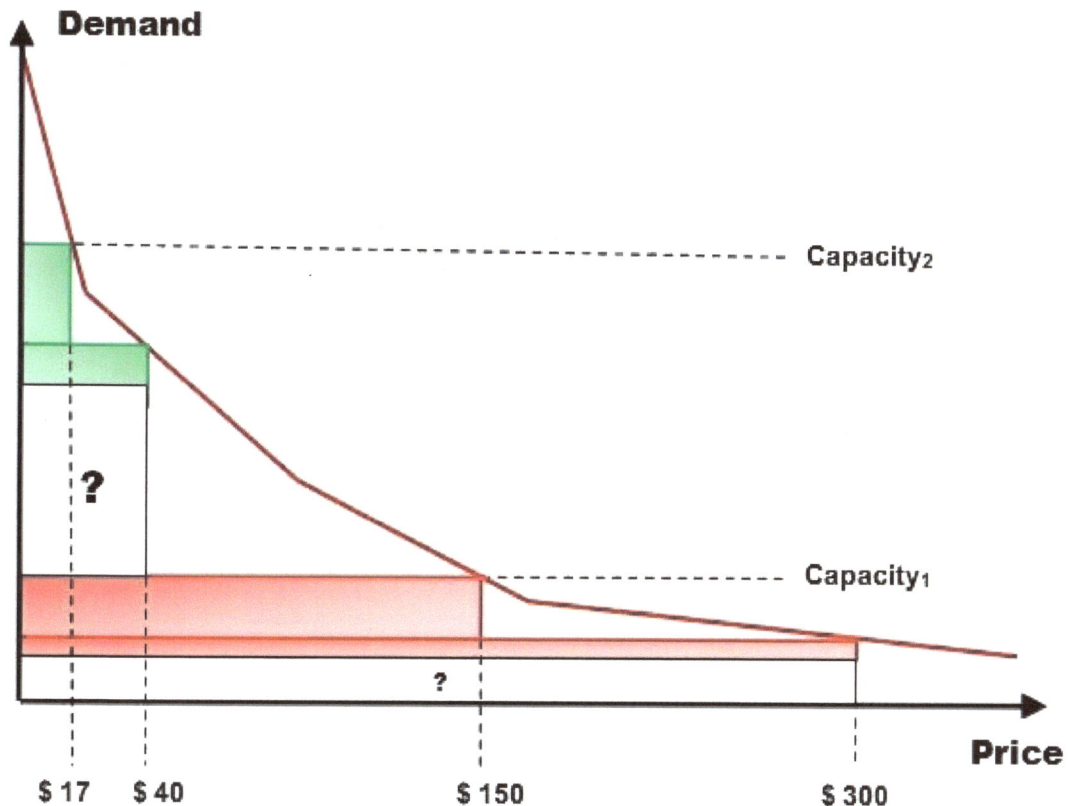

<u>Solution:</u>
The broken four-segment straight line used by the railroad company seems to be not an appropriate approximation of the actual Demand = f(Price) market curve. A system of dynamic pricing should be certainly more adequate.

Appendix

Here are some screens of a computer assisted system defining the selling prices:

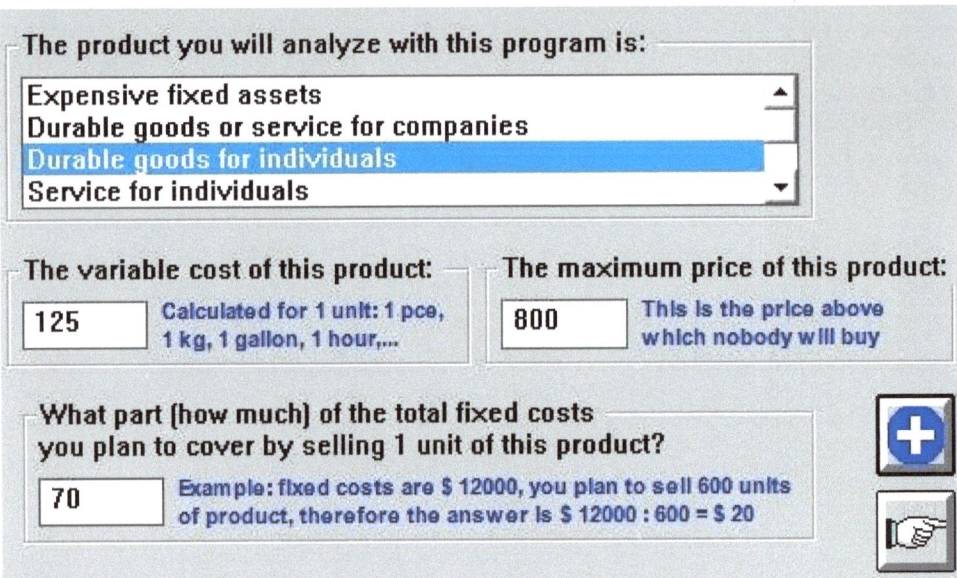

Data concerning the product which has to be priced: the calculation of P_{BE} as well as P_0 will be performed here.

Please specify the perceived by customers quality as well as the selling price for each of your product active competitors:

	lower	= as ours	higher		
Competitor 1 - quality:				, sell. price:	319
Competitor 2 - quality:				, sell. price:	379
Competitor 3 - quality:				, sell. price:	439
Competitor 4 - quality:				, sell. price:	0

The shift of the scroll bar from the center must be proportional to the perceived quality
In case your product has no competitors, please do not answer the above questions

What is the market share of the analyzed product?

15 %   Please, try to evaluate considering all present on the market competitors

Data concerning the competition allow calculation of P_H.

What will be your strategy related to the analyzed product?

☐ Market penetration (low price, progressively increasing)

☐ Skimming (high price, progressively reducing)

☐ Maximization of market share

☑ Maximization of profit and cash-flow

☐ Mass market (price low compared to competition)

☐ Differentiation of product (price high compared to competition)

☐ A fast clean out of inventories is required

What is the stage of life cycle of product?

Introduction on market
Growth
Maturity

Please, choose one from these 4

The inflation is:

| 0 - 5 ▼ | % |

per year

A planned price evolution in the future.

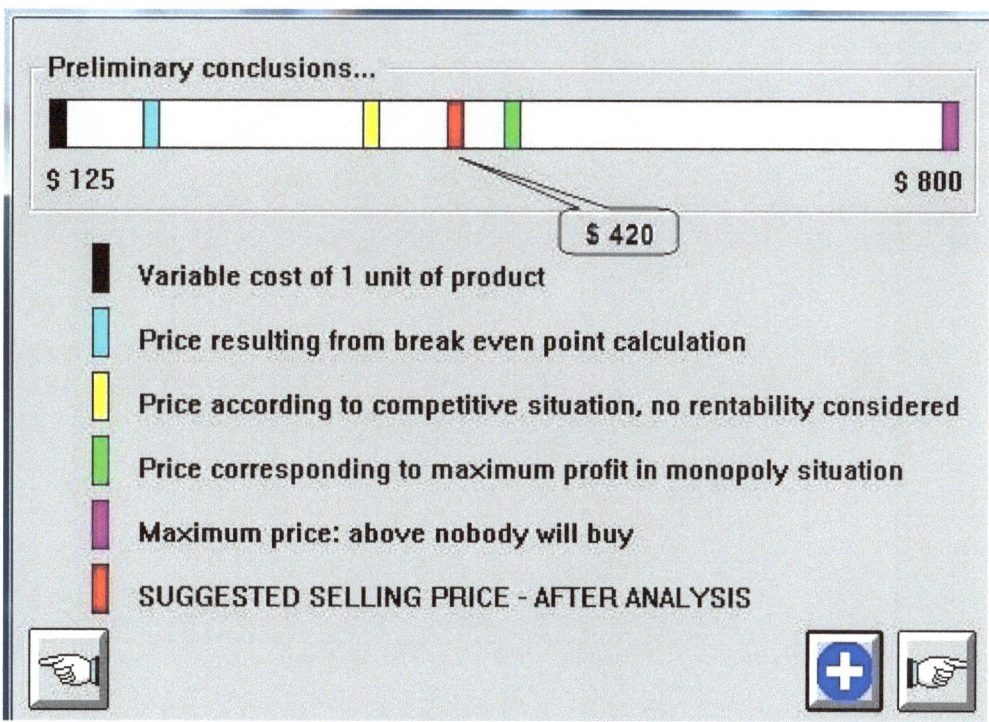

Preliminary conclusions...

$ 125 $ 800

$ 420

▮ Variable cost of 1 unit of product

▯ Price resulting from break even point calculation

▯ Price according to competitive situation, no rentability considered

▯ Price corresponding to maximum profit in monopoly situation

▮ Maximum price: above nobody will buy

▮ SUGGESTED SELLING PRICE - AFTER ANALYSIS

Final results: the suggested selling price is $ 420.

Index

Break even point 10, 16, 21
Competitors 12
Conjoint analysis 23
Capacity reservation 31
Demand curve 8, 13, 25
Discounts 20
Dynamic pricing 33
Elasticity 14
Fencing 25, 31, 33
Fluctuation of demand 28, 31, 33
Honest price 12, 16, 21
Luxury product 8
Market point of view 8
Maximum demand 9, 14
Maximum price 9
Optimum price 11, 16, 21
Penetration 17
Output capacity 24
Popular product 8
Price barriers (thresholds) 21
Price differentiation 25
Profitability 9
Protection level 31
Quality 3, 12
Reservation curve 33
Revenue management 29
Screaming 17
Yield management 29

Author

Michel Muszynski is graduated from European Institute of Business Administration (INSEAD). His career began in the marketing high-tech in Applied Research Laboratories (the branch of Bausch and Lomb) in France and then in Beckman in Switzerland. In 1982 he became appointed as manager of international applications in Instruments S.A. in USA, and since 1988 held the position of general manager of MVE S.A. (branch of DANONE) in France. In 1990, he started in Warsaw and was the dean of the department of Institut Français de Gestion - the school of management based in Paris, running management postgraduate programs and delivering the diploma of Master of Business Administration.

Professor Muszynski lives in Paris as well as in Miami (Florida) and is expert of strategic management. He is also author of about 200 publications devoted to this subject and specialist of computer assisted management. In 1990 he published in France one of first in the world manuals of the artificial intelligence applied in business („Conduire une entreprise avec un système-expert") and in 2006, in the United States, the book "Corporate strategy – an interactive approach" and then "Interactive business simulations – e-learning and more". He also published in Poland the book "Why companies fail?" as well as "44 hair raising stories for managers". Professor Muszynski is the author of over thirty strategic computer didactic simulation programs and inventor of the unique method of teaching business with their use (now in four lingual versions). He also realized and published „Multimedia Encyclopedia of Management" on cd-rom.

To contact the author: info@simulations-for-education.com